Men

and Other Reptiles

Men

and Other Reptiles

CB
CONTEMPORARY
BOOKS
CHICAGO

Library of Congress
Cataloging-in-Publication Data

Men and other reptiles.
    p. cm.
   ISBN 0-8092-3784-9
   1. Men—Quotations, maxims, etc.
   2. Men—Humor.
PN6084.M4M46 1993
305.31—dc20   93-22078
                     CIP

Published by Contemporary Books, Inc.
180 North Michigan Avenue, Chicago,
   Illinois 60601
Manufactured in the United States of
   America
International Standard Book Number:
   0-8092-3784-9

To
Alan, Andrew, Arlen, Bill, Bob,
Christopher, Chuck, Clarence,
Dan, Dave, David, Frank, Gary,
George, Greg, Harold, Henry, J.
Eugene, Jack, James, John, Keith,
Kent, Lawrence, Mark, Michael,
Ned, Patrick, Paul, Peter, Philip,
Richard, Ron, Samuel, Sean, Sig-
mund, Steve, Vincent, Wally . . .
and, most of all, to

_____

(Your Reptile Here)

Men

and Other Reptiles

Women want mediocre men, and men are working hard to be as mediocre as possible.
—*Margaret Mead*

I keep hearing that there's a new breed of men out there who don't talk about helping a woman as though they're doing you a favor and who do seriously consider leaving the office if a child comes down with a fever at school, rather than assuming that you will leave yours. But from what I've seen, there aren't enough of these men to qualify as a breed, only as a subgroup.
—*Anna Quindlen,*
Living Out Loud

1

Because men are simple, they are not physically capable of handling more than one task at a time. Women can easily cook dinner, feed the baby, and talk on the phone all at once. Were a man to try this, he would probably explode.

—*Roseanne Arnold*

Men will always opt for things that get finished and stay that way—putting up screens, but not planning menus.

—*Jane O'Reilly*

A man is *so* in the way in the house.
— *Mrs. Gaskell*

Women don't get hung up making deals the way men do.
— *Shirley Chisholm*

Do not put such unlimited power into the hands of husbands. Remember, all men would be tyrants if they could.
— *Abigail Adams*

The fact is that men need women more than women need men; and so, aware of this fact, man has sought to keep woman dependent upon him economically as the only method open to him of making himself necessary to her.

—*Elizabeth Gould Davis*,
The First Sex

Men have always been afraid that women could get along without them.

—*Margaret Mead*

Oh, you're incredible, utterly incredible, perched up on that pinnacle of masculine ego, looking down at poor, weak, defenseless females—and pitying them because they don't have beards.

> —*Bette Davis as Linda Gilman to Robert Montgomery as Casey Jackson in* June Bride

Trust your husband, adore your husband, and get as much as you can in your own name.

> —*Joan Rivers*

I wish I had been born a man. . . . The concerns are so simple: money and death.

—*Katharine Hepburn as*
Agnes in A Delicate Balance

We seem to have a great nostalgia for the good old days—"when men were men"—or so we think. . . . We have greatly romanticized this picture. It was so much easier for a man to look masculine when women were subservient.

—*Eda Le Shan,*
How to Survive Parenthood

If there is anything disagreeable going on, men are sure to get out of it.

—*Jane Austen,*
Northanger Abbey

QUESTION: What's a man's idea of helping you with the housework?
ANSWER: Lifting his legs so you can vacuum.

I married beneath me—all women do.

—*Nancy Astor*

The fundamental reason that women do not achieve so greatly as men do is that women have no wives.

—*Professor Marjorie Nicholson*, Reader's Digest, *1941*

Anyone who believes that men and women have the same mindset hasn't lived on earth. A man thinks that everything he does is wonderful; a woman has *doubts*.

—*Margo Kaufman*

I never married because there was no need. I have three pets at home which answer the same purpose as a husband. I have a dog which growls every morning, a parrot which swears all afternoon, and a cat that comes home late at night.

—*Marie Corelli*

Personally, I think if a woman hasn't met the right man by the time she's twenty-four, she may be lucky.

—*Deborah Kerr*,
   Women's Wit and Wisdom

Take care of him. Make him feel important. If you can do that, you'll have a happy and wonderful marriage—like two out of every ten couples.

—*Mildred Natwick as Ethel Banks to Jane Fonda as Corie Bratter in* Barefoot in the Park

The hardest task in a girl's life is to prove to a man that his intentions are serious.

—*Helen Rowland*

I'd like to get married because I like the idea of a man being required by law to sleep with me every night.

—*Carrie Snow*

Woman wants monogamy;
Man delights in novelty.

—*Dorothy Parker,*
Enough Rope

Although man has learned through evolution to walk in an upright position, his eyes still swing from limb to limb.

—*Margaret Schooley*

QUESTION: How do men exercise at the beach?

ANSWER: By sucking in their stomachs every time they see a bikini.

All men are led by one thing, and that's their willy.

—*Shirlie, of Pepsi and Shirlie*

It is funny the two things most men are proudest of is the thing that any man can do and does in the same way, that is being drunk and being the father of their son.

—*Gertrude Stein*

Men will talk, sometimes in complete sentences but more often not, to women on the street. In my case, I hear a lot of "Yo, Red!" Exactly what am I supposed to do with a comment like Yo, Red? Yell back "Yo, Bald!" or "Yo, Short!"?

—*Dorian Yeager*

A man admires the woman who makes him think, but he keeps away from her. He likes the woman who makes him laugh. He loves the girl who hurts him. But he marries the woman who flatters him.

—*Nellie B. Stull,*
Reader's Digest, *1935*

No, Mother, I haven't met Mr. Right yet . . . but I have met Mr. Cheap, Mr. Rude, and Mr. Married.

—*T-shirt*

I sometimes think what men really want now is a sexually experienced virgin.

—*Anonymous*

When he said we were trying to make a fool of him, I could only murmur that the Creator had beat us to it.

—*Ilka Chase*

If a man is vain, flatter. If timid, flatter. If boastful, flatter. In all history, too much flattery never lost a gentlemen.

—*Kathryn Cravens,*
Pursuit of Gentlemen

That the most intelligent, discerning, and learned men, men of talent and feeling, should finally put all their pride in their crotch, as awed as they are uneasy at the few inches sticking out in front of them, proves how normal it is for the world to be crazy.

—*Françoise Parturier,*
Open Letter to Men

In men this blunder still you find,—
All think their little set mankind.

> —*Hannah More*,
> Florio and His Friend

I wonder why men can get serious at all. They have this delicate, long thing hanging outside their bodies, which goes up and down by its own will. . . . If I were a man I would always be laughing at myself.

> —*Yoko Ono*, Grapefruit

A good many men still like to think of their wives as they do of their religion: neglected but always there.

—*Freya Stark,*
The Journey's Echo

Real equality is going to come not when a female Einstein is recognized as quickly as a male Einstein but when a female schlemiel is promoted as quickly as a male schlemiel.

—*Bella Abzug*

Reason #726 Why Dogs Are Better than Men:
No Dog Ever Voted to Confirm Clarence Thomas.

—*T-shirt*

Some men haven't the brains of a gopher about what's appropriate to say and whom to say it to in the workplace.

—*Helen Gurley Brown*

The surest way to be alone is to get married.

—*Gloria Steinem*

A bachelor never gets over the idea that he is a thing of beauty and a boy forever.

— *Helen Rowland*

Men are beasts, and even beasts don't behave as they do.

— *Brigitte Bardot*

Very few men care to have the obvious pointed out to them by a woman.

— *Margaret Baillie Saunders,*
A Shepherd of Kensington

QUESTION: How do men define a
50/50 relationship?
ANSWER: You cook/they eat;
you clean/they dirty; you
iron/they wrinkle.

There are not many males, black
or white, who wish to get in-
volved with a woman who's committed to her own development.
—*Eleanor Holmes Norton*

QUESTION: How do you get a
man to exercise?
ANSWER: Put the remote control
between his feet.

QUESTION: Why is it good that there are female astronauts?

ANSWER: Because when the crew gets lost in space, at least a woman will ask for directions.

Oddly enough, while men cannot remember basic facts—like your dress size or your anniversary—they can recite from memory every statistic from every football game that took place during the last six years.

—*Roseanne Arnold*

It's been my experience that men who say they believe in 50/50 relationships are prone to telling half-truths.

—*Anonymous*

Women see differently than men. If you doubt this, I would merely remind you of the last time a male walked into a room that looked as though it had been ransacked by hostile—and profoundly sloppy—foreign agents and innocently uttered the words "What mess?"

—*Dorian Yeager*

I'm not implying that all men are blowhards, bores, cads, creeps, geeks, tightwads, or your all-around generic jerks. But odds are, you will have to date an assortment of the above before finding someone who rates higher than a 2 on the human being scale.

—*Audrey Norris*

Let's face it: Brains and boys just don't mix. Okay, some guys do find staggering intelligence a turn-on, but most will take the twit over the wit any night of the week.

—*Nina Malkin*

I don't know where this myth comes from, that women are neat and tidy and men are slobs. The men I have known have been, by and large, a fairly prissy bunch, prone to uttering such inanities as "If a thing is worth doing, it's worth doing well."

—*Adair Lara*

There are many words you could use to describe men. You could say they are loving, kind, considerate. You'd be wrong, but you could say them.

—*Anonymous*

I fear nothing so much as a man who is witty all day long.
    —*Mme de Sévigné*

You can talk to a man about any subject. He won't understand, but you can talk to him.
    —*Anonymous*

The usual masculine disillusionment is in discovering that a woman has a brain.
    —*Margaret Mitchell,*
    Gone with the Wind

Why is woman persistently regarded as a mystery? It is not that she has labored to conceal the organic and psychological facts of her constitution but that men have showed no interest in exploring them.

—*Ruth Herschberger*,
Adam's Rib

I'd be willing to bet that if one day a woman walked barefoot to the moon and back and a man cleaned out his desk, when the two of them sat down to dinner that night, he would groan, "Boy, was that desk a mess."

—*Margo Kaufman*

We do not ask man to represent us; it is hard enough in times like these for man to carry backbone enough to represent himself.

—*Elizabeth Cady Stanton, 1860*

Men are nothing but lazy lumps of drunken flesh. They crowd you in bed, get you all worked up, and then before you can say, "Is that all there is?," that's all there is.

—*Mrs. Gravas (Latka's mother) on "Taxi"*

It is impossible to rely on the prudence or common sense of any man.
—*Mrs. Alexander,*
    Ralph Wilton's Weird, *1875*

Never trust a husband too far, nor a bachelor too near.
—*Helen Rowland,*
    The Rubaiyat of a Bachelor,
    1915

Whenever you want to marry someone, go have lunch with his ex-wife.
—*Shelley Winters*

It is ridiculous to think you can spend your entire life with one person. Three is about the right number. Yes, I imagine three husbands would do it.

—*Clare Boothe Luce*

Whatever women do they must do twice as well as men to be thought half as good. Luckily, this is not difficult.

—*Charlotte Whitton*

Not all women are fools. Some are single.

—*bumper sticker*

A man expects his wife to be perfect—and to understand why he isn't.

—*Anonymous*

Women have their faults
Men have only two
Everything they say
And everything they do.

—*Anonymous*

QUESTION: Why are all dumb-blond jokes one-liners?
ANSWER: So men can understand them.

Men themselves sabotage our best intentions. Someone you've seen only in a simple but attractive blue suit will arrive at your door in plaid pants and an aqua turtleneck. A man you thought had taste will take you to Fatso's Pasta for an all-you-can-eat, $2.99 spaghetti special. . . . Yet another turns out to believe that every woman's secret desire is to have the fine points of football demonstrated with the silverware.

—*Jane Campbell*

The softer a man's head, the louder his socks.

—*Helen Rowland*

If you cannot have your dear husband for a comfort and a delight, for a breadwinner and a crosspatch, for a sofa, a chair, or a hot-water bottle, one can use him as a cross to be borne.

—*Florence Margaret (Stevie) Smith*

Blessed is the man who, having nothing to say, abstains from giving in words evidence of the fact.

—*George Eliot (Mary Ann Evans)*

Man's role is uncertain, unde-
fined, and perhaps unnecessary.
By a great effort man has hit
upon a method of compensating
himself for his basic inferiority.
                    —*Margaret Mead*

You're not too smart. I like that
in a man.
          —*Kathleen Turner as Matty
          Walker to William Hurt
          as Ned Racine in* Body
          Heat

QUESTION: Why is psychoanalysis so much quicker for men than for women?

ANSWER: Because when it's time to go back to childhood, he's already there.

The follies which a man regrets most in his life are those which he didn't commit when he had the opportunity.

—*Helen Rowland,*
   Reflections of a Bachelor Girl

I wouldn't trust my husband with a young woman for five minutes, and he's been dead for twenty-five years.

—*Brendan Behan's mother*

Have you ever noticed that what passes as a terrific man would only be an adequate woman?

—*Anna Quindlen,*
Living Out Loud

By the time most men learn how to behave themselves, they are too old to do anything else.

—*Anonymous*

There ain't nothin' an ol' man can do but bring me a message from a young one.

—*Jackie "Moms" Mabley*

At twenty, a man feels awfully aged and blasé; at thirty, almost senile; at forty, "not so old"; at fifty, positively skittish.

—*Helen Rowland*

I like men to behave like men— strong and childish.

—*Françoise Sagan*

A man's home may seem to be his castle on the outside; inside it is more often his nursery.
—*Clare Booth Luce,*
  Women's Wit and Wisdom

Much male fear of feminism is infantilism—the longing to remain the mother's son, to possess a woman who exists purely for him. These infantile needs of adult men for women have been sentimentalized and romanticized long enough as "love"; it is time to recognize them as arrested development.
—*Adrienne Rich*

Men don't get smarter when they grow older. They just lose their hair.

—*Claudette Colbert as Gerry Jeffers in* The Palm Beach Story

When a man falls in love with himself, it is the beginning of a lifelong romance.

—*Anonymous*

It should be a very happy marriage—they are both so much in love with *him*.

—*Irene Thomas*

THEY HAD TO TAKE A POLL?
(PART I)

On average, today's man spends forty-five minutes each day on personal grooming, up from thirty minutes a day in 1988.
—GQ, *1990*

. . . .

Forty-two percent of the women polled . . . believed men are basically selfish and self-centered—up from 32 percent in 1970.
—*Roper Organization, 1990*

It is always incomprehensible to a man that a woman should ever refuse an offer of marriage.

—*Jane Austen*

When a man can't explain a woman's actions, the first thing he thinks about is the condition of her uterus.

—*Clare Boothe Luce,*
Slam the Door Softly

Men have always detested women's gossip because they suspect the truth: their measurements are being taken and compared.

—*Erica Jong*

He is every other inch a gentle-
man.

—Rebecca West

"Men's stuff?" Lord have mercy!
Get out my spinning wheel,
girls. I'll join the harem section
in a minute.

—Elizabeth Taylor as Leslie
Lynnton in Giant

HUSBAND: What can I do to
    make sex better for you?
WIFE: Leave town.

Can you imagine a world without men? No crime and lots of happy, fat women.
—*Marion Smith*

If you are living with a man, you don't have to worry about whether you should sleep with him after dinner.
—*Stephanie Brush*

Where's the man could ease a heart like a satin gown?
—*Dorothy Parker,*
   Not So Deep As a Well, *1936*

The average man takes all the natural taste out of his food by covering it with ready-made sauces, and all the personality out of a woman by covering her with his ready-made ideals.

—*Helen Rowland,*
A Guide to Men

Men have structured society to make a woman feel guilty if she looks after herself. Well, I beat men at their own game. I don't look down on men, but I certainly don't look up to them either. I never found a man I could love—or trust—the way I loved myself.

—*Mae West*

HUSBAND: Let's go out and have some fun tonight.

WIFE: All right, but if you get home before I do, leave the door unlocked.

How do I feel about men? With my fingers!

—*Cher*

Woman's virtue is man's greatest invention.

—*Cornelia Otis Skinner*

Women have served all these centuries as looking-glasses possessing the magic and delicious power of reflecting the figure of man at twice its natural size.
— *Virginia Woolf,*
A Room of One's Own

The next time the man in your life accuses you of having no sense of humor, sweetly remind him that you are the one responsible for handling the gnarly issues of contraception.
— *Dorian Yeager*

As long as you know that most men are like children, you know everything.

—*attributed to Coco Chanel*

Men are more conventional than women and slower to change their ideas.

—*Kathleen Norris,*
Hands Full of Living

A man has only one escape from his old self: to see a different self—in the mirror of some woman's eyes.

—*Clare Booth Luce,*
The Women

Straight men don't have time to spend with you because they have to get laid.

—*Bette Midler*

A man may talk inspiringly to a woman about love in the abstract—but the look in his eyes is always perfectly concrete.

—*Helen Rowland*

QUESTION: What's the definition of marriage?
ANSWER: A ceremony that turns your dream boat into a barge.

Give a man a free hand, and he'll run it all over you.

—*Mae West*

Men are those creatures with two legs and eight hands.

—*Jayne Mansfield*

We were walking down the street. He looked into another girl's eyes, and just fell madly in love. She was wearing mirrored sunglasses.

—*Rita Rudner*

The advantage of being married to an archaeologist is that the older one grows the more interested he becomes.

—*Agatha Christie,*
    Murder in Mesopotamia

When he is late for dinner and I know he must be either having an affair or lying dead on the street, I always hope he's dead.

—*Judith Viorst,*
    Women's Wit and Wisdom

Husbands are like fires. They go out when unattended.

—*Zsa Zsa Gabor*

QUESTION: What's the difference between a man and E.T.?
ANSWER: E.T. phoned home.

It is easier to keep half a dozen lovers guessing than to keep one lover after he has stopped guessing.

—*Helen Rowland*

No nice men are good at getting taxis.

—*Katharine Whitehorn*

Man is kind only to be cruel; woman cruel only to be kind.
> —*Minna Antrim, 1902*

Men don't know anything about pain; they've never experienced labor, cramps, or a bikini wax.
> —*Nan Tisdale,* Self

It's no news to women that male attractiveness is judged in a different light from women's. Sometimes, it would seem, in total darkness.
> —*Dorian Yeager*

QUESTION: How do you get an ex-boyfriend out of a tree?
ANSWER: Cut the rope.

I'd rather pay a young man's fare to California than tell an ol' man the distance.

—*Jackie "Moms" Mabley*

Don't accept rides from strange men—and remember that all men are as strange as hell.

—*Robin Morgan,*
Sisterhood Is Powerful

Men have no experience "taking hints." Your attempts at subtlety—which work so well with your female friends—will get you nowhere with your husbands.

—*Roseanne Arnold*

All men should be sent to an island where they can walk around in ripped underwear and drink milk out of a carton until they drop.

—*Susan Dey as Wally on "Love and War"*

Men cook when attention will be paid. They don't cook on ordinary nights, when three people besides themselves are hungry.
—*Leslie Newman*

Nothing is more debasing for a real man than a plastic apron.
—*Lady Lewisham*

QUESTION: What is a man's idea of a seven-course meal?
ANSWER: A hot dog and a six-pack.

There are so many kinds of awful men.
  —*Wendy Cope*, Making Cocoa
    for Kingsley Amis

The fantasy of every Australian man is to have two women—one cleaning and the other dusting.
                    —*Maureen Murphy*

When you see what some girls marry, you realize how they must hate to work for a living.
  —*Helen Rowland*, Reflections
    of a Bachelor Girl, *1903*

Southern men have their own brand of macho. All that sugar-sugar and gallantry can be a way of dominating and manipulating women. Southern men view women as frail, delicate, wispy creatures prone to bouts of blushing, fainting, and attacks of the vapors. It's a traditional thing.

—*Reported in* Playgirl *magazine*

Nothing annoys a man as much as to hear a woman promising to love him "forever" when he merely wanted her to love him for a few weeks.

—*Helen Rowland*

Who is my Mr. Right? Will I ever find him? Does he even exist? Is there such a creature as Mr. Right? How did this searching for Mr. Right get started, anyway?

—*Gwen Lehmann*

QUESTION: What's the difference between a man and a hot fudge sundae?

ANSWER: A hot fudge sundae will satisfy a woman every time.

The more I see of men, the more I like dogs.

—*Mme de Staël*

A man has to be Joe McCarthy to be called ruthless. All a woman has to do is put you on hold.

—*Marlo Thomas*,
Women's Wit and Wisdom

Not all women give most of their waking thoughts to the problem of pleasing men. Some are married.

—*Emma Lee*

THERAPIST: Why don't you try using a little imagination when you make love to your husband?

WIFE: You mean imagine it's good?

It is a truth universally acknowledged, that a single man in possession of a good fortune must be in want of a wife.

—*Jane Austen,*
Pride and Prejudice

He's the kind of man a woman would have to marry to get rid of.

—*Mae West*

Love is like playing checkers. You have to know which man to move.

—*Jackie "Moms" Mabley*

A man in love is incomplete until he is married. Then he's finished.

—*Zsa Zsa Gabor*

Before marriage a man will lie awake all night thinking about something you said; after marriage he will fall asleep before you have finished saying it.
—*Helen Rowland*

There is so little difference between husbands you might as well keep the first.
—*Adela Rogers St. Johns*

A man—despite some similarities—is not like dog droppings. For one thing, he's probably too big to just step over.

—*Dorian Yeager*

QUESTION: Do you know what it means when you come home to a little affection, a little tenderness, and a little sympathy?

ANSWER: It means you're in the wrong house.

PROVERBIAL WISDOM

Lying will marry you a wife, but it won't keep her.
> —*West Africa (Fulani)*

. . . .

A man in love schemes more than a hundred lawyers.
> —*Spain*

. . . .

A man who's too good for this world is no good for his wife.
> —*Yiddish*

When a man makes a mistake in his first marriage, the victim is his second wife.

—*Anonymous*

I want a man who's kind and understanding. Is that too much to ask of a millionaire?

—*Zsa Zsa Gabor*

Man forgives woman anything save the wit to outwit him.

—*Minna Antrim, 1902*

A man finds out what is meant
by a spitting image when he tries
to feed cereal to his infant.
—*Imogene Fey*

What is the use of being a little
boy if you are going to grow up
to be a man?
—*Gertrude Stein*

One cannot be always laughing
at a man without now and then
stumbling on something witty.
—*Jane Austen,*
Pride and Prejudice

I don't believe man is woman's natural enemy. Perhaps his lawyer is.

—*Shana Alexander*

Sometimes I wonder if men and women really suit each other. Perhaps they should live next door and just visit now and then.

—*Katharine Hepburn,*
Women's Wit and Wisdom

Valuable books, they are almost as rare as valuable men.

—*Mary Wortley Montagu*

QUESTION: How many men does it take to change a light bulb?
ANSWER: Five. One to force it with a hammer and four to go out for more bulbs.

Oh, *l'amour, l'amour* . . . how it *can* let you down.
—*Mary Boland as the Countess De Lave (Flora), en route to Reno for a quick divorce in* The Women

Women, it is true, make human beings, but only men can make men.

—*Margaret Mead*

Adam's rib simply isn't the sedate sanctum that it once was. Eve's pill has changed all that.

—*Senator Margaret Chase Smith, 1969*

It's not the men in your life that count. It's the life in your men.

—*Mae West*

AND NOW, A WORD FROM OUR TARGETS

Men have a much better time of it than women. For one thing, they marry later. For another thing, they die earlier.

     —*H. L. Mencken*

Every man over forty is a scoundrel.

     —*George Bernard Shaw*

The tragedy of man is that he can conceive self-perfection but cannot achieve it.

—*Reinhold Niebuhr*

No man is a man until his father tells him he is—I was forty-eight.

—*Burt Reynolds*

A man is in general better pleased when he has a good dinner upon his table than when his wife talks Greek.

—*Samuel Johnson,*
Miscellanies

I tended to place my wife under a pedestal.

—*Woody Allen*

The real problem is not whether machines think, but whether men do.

—*B. F. Skinner*

There's a great woman behind every idiot.

—*John Lennon*

It's just as hard for man to break the habit of thinking of himself as central to the species as it was to break the habit of thinking of himself as central to the universe.

—*Elaine Morgan,*
The Descent of Woman

You will never, never believe me—I can hardly believe it myself—but guys actually tell me they will respect you more in the morning if you don't sleep with them on the first date.

—*Karen Donnelly*

QUESTION: Why did Dorothy get lost in Oz?

ANSWER: She had three men giving her directions.

I'm probably not the only woman in the world who has discovered that her mate—the one for whom she has forsaken all others—is *just like* all others.

—*Laura Billings*

A husband is what is left of the lover after the nerve has been extracted.

—*Helen Rowland,*
A Guide to Men

In evolutionary terms, females are more advanced than males. Women are more human than men.

—*Anthropologist Ashley Montagu*, The Natural Superiority of Women

Why is it that whenever you try to have an intelligent conversation with an important man in your life, his eyes glaze over like a three-day-old mackerel's?

—Playgirl *magazine*

Middle-aged *rabbits* don't have a paunch, do have their own teeth, and haven't lost their romantic appeal.

—*Aurelia Potor*

The true male never yet walked
Who liked to listen when his
   mate talked.
—*Anna Wickham*, The Affinity

I think the men's movement is a great idea. I just wish part of the movement they made was to clean the bathtub.

—*Anonymous*

Whatever happened to the strong, silent type? Today's man talks, talks, talks 'til we're blue in the face. And I fear there's no undoing the damage. The new old saying? Boys will be noise.

—*Nina Malkin*

QUESTION: What makes men chase women they have no intention of marrying?

ANSWER: The same urge that makes dogs chase cars they have no intention of driving.

We probably all fantasize about being pursued by a tall, dark, handsome man. But take it from me: When the guy has the depth of a dime and the sensitivity of Mount Rushmore, it's no fun.

—*Robin Westen*

When two people marry they become, in the eyes of the law, one person, and that one person is the husband!

—*Shana Alexander*

Men rarely seem to assume they've made a mistake.

—*Margo Kaufman*

Show me a man in designer jeans and I'll show you a man whose mother dressed him funny.

—*attributed to Charo*

Anytime a man tells you he's a hopeless romantic, you can bet he's simply hopeless.

—*Anonymous*

If either gender can be labeled "romance junkies," it's men. They fall in love faster and more often than we do.

—*Shelley Levitt*

QUESTION: What single word best describes most men in singles bars?
ANSWER: Married.

Show me a young man who actively embraces Republicanism and I'll show you the world's most boring date.

—*Stevie Simels*

The male always seems to be discovering a cure for something, no matter what he's doing.

—*Margo Kaufman*

Why did Catherine the Great have her lovers killed after one night of sex? Because she couldn't stand the empty feeling when a lover didn't telephone the next day.

—*Gael Greene*, Delicious Sex

Stage fright notwithstanding, one must wonder what possesses a man while he utters the most inane comment ever verbalized as a way of introducing himself.

—*Dorian Yeager*

Top Ten
Worst Pick-Up Lines

1. Is it hot in here, or is it you?
2. Can you buy me a drink?
3. Will you be the mother of my children?
4. Didn't we meet in a past life?
5. Can I make you breakfast tomorrow morning?
6. If I told you you had a nice body, would you hold it against me?
7. Didn't I see you in *Penthouse* magazine?
8. Aren't you a little old to be in a bar like this?
9. Do I look like a married man to you?
10. I'm with the phone company. Can I reach out and touch you?

According to Professor William Gwen of Texas A & M University, men are less able than women to distinguish love from related emotions.

—*Reported in* Playgirl *magazine*

We were six ladies at dinner this evening. No men. We had a free and cheery time.

—*Elizabeth Cady Stanton*

I didn't leave Sonny for another man. I left him for another woman—me. I was choking.

—*Cher*

As far as a man is concerned, the only acceptable reason to leave him is if you're in love with another man. Anything else—such as your desire to get out from under a guy's thumb and just be yourself—is considered an act of treason against the Boys' Club.

—*Anonymous*

QUESTION: Why is a dog man's best friend?
ANSWER: Because a dog won't tell on him.

When he's sick, she nourishes him back to health. When she's sick, well, she can't stay sick for long.

—*Daphne Simkins,*
Chicago Tribune

QUESTION: What's the fastest way to lose 180 ugly pounds?
ANSWER: Throw the bum out.

The hard thing is when you love him and he loves you, but because of whatever problem he has, he can't allow himself to be happy.

—*Morgan Fairchild*

The fact that women with the most education don't get married should have been the tip-off. They *know* better.
—*Chelsea Munroe*

When a man comes home snarling after a bad day at work, when he doesn't lift a finger in the kitchen, when he's snoring on the couch by nine, the last thing I feel toward him is sexual. He calls this "withholding" or "manipulative." I call it natural.
—*Pamela Redmond Satran*

If you watch "The Honeymooners" regularly, you will learn everything you ever need to know about getting along with a man. Alice Kramden is a genius.

—*Stephanie Brush*

You only have to wonder, "Whatever did I see in him?" to realize that what you saw must have been a product of your own imagination.

—*Allie Walmsley*

It isn't tying himself to one woman that a man dreads when he thinks of marrying; it's separating himself from all the others.

—*Helen Rowland*

QUESTION: How many men does it take to change a light bulb?
ANSWER: None. Every man knows that if he puts it off long enough, a woman will take care of it.

I don't like a man who looks you over and scrutinizes you. This is not sexy.

—*Goldie Hawn*

Older women don't kid themselves. An older woman knows a younger man will see her body and his pulse won't exactly race. So what does an older man think when a younger woman wants to date him? It's obvious—he's a love machine.

—*Estelle Getty*

Older men are boring old farts who fall asleep after a hard day at the office. Who wants that?

—*Cher*

When the government (mostly men) gets together to legislate "what is good for women," the result is usually less than beneficial.

—*Candida Royalle*

Men are the speedbumps on the highway of life.

—*Anonymous*

QUESTION: What's the difference between a new dog and a new husband?
ANSWER: After a year, the dog is still excited to see you.

Is it possible to have a committed, monogamous relationship forever? Or is it simply in a man's nature—something deep and murky and inexplicable—to be a lying, philandering horse's ass?

—*Traci Johnson*

He said, "Well, you know, Paula, a lot of guys think you're gay." I don't know if that was supposed to be a compelling reason for me to sleep with him. I guess he somehow thought that if I slept with him, he would sign an affidavit and show it to fellows so that they would indeed know that I was obviously able to participate.

—*Paula Poundstone*

The definition of masculinity is eighty-twenty, or sixty-forty, male to female, so if you propose fifty-fifty, or behave fifty-fifty, that's a real threat to some men's identity.

—*Gloria Steinem*

Unless your mate goes by the name of "John-Boy," chances are he spent his entire childhood mastering the fine art of chore avoidance. This is the essential male pastime, on which all of those lesser avocations—fishing, Monday Night Football, global imperialism—are founded.

—*Aaron Gell*

It's true that girls are often inclined to marry men like their fathers, which explains why so many mothers cry at weddings.

—*Anonymous*

QUESTION: What does the word *macho* stand for?
ANSWER: Men Avoiding Chores at Home and Outside

Boy meets girl. Boy asks for girl's number. Boy says he'll call. Boy never does. What *is* it that always happens between "I'll call you later" and later?

—*Lynn Reich*

He certainly seemed like Mr. Right when we met. But if I met him now I'd run away screaming.

—*Anonymous*

Every man wants a woman to appeal to his better side, his nobler instincts, and his higher nature—and another woman to help him forget them.

—*Helen Rowland,*
A Guide to Men

Men like us to look good, as long as they don't have to know how we got that way. It's as if men feel cheated in some way when they discover that being a vision of loveliness takes work.

—*Nina Malkin*

Men are always so annoyingly sure of themselves—even when they have no right to be.
—*Gwen Lehmann*

Men seem to face bullets, napalm, and the average American garage mechanic with stoic equanimity. Total honesty, however, has been known to reduce the most macho of the species to a lump of quivering protoplasm.
—*Dorian Yeager*

Marrying a man is like buying something you've been admiring for a long time in a shop window. You may love it when you get it home, but it doesn't always go with everything else in the house.

—*Jean Kerr,*
   The Snake Has All the Lines

There's nothing so stubborn as a man when you want him to do something.

—*Jean Giradoux,*
   The Madwoman of Chaillot

The best way to get most husbands to do something is to suggest that perhaps they're too old to do it.

—*Shirley MacLaine*

QUESTION: Why do lawyers make lousy lovers?
ANSWER: They're always objecting.

. . . .

QUESTION: Why do bankers make great lovers?
ANSWER: They know there's a substantial penalty for early withdrawal.

Men are idiots, and I married their king.

—*Katey Sagal as Peg Bundy on "Married with Children"*

My husband is a jolly good sort, one of those very hearty men. He wears plus fours, smokes a long pipe, and talks about nothing but beer and rugby football. My nerves won't stand much more of it.

—*a wife at Tottenham police court*

THEY HAD TO TAKE A POLL?
(PART II)

Fifty percent of the women polled by the Roper Organization agreed that men are more interested in their own, rather than a woman's, sexual satisfaction—up from 40 percent in 1970.

—Ladies' Home Journal, *1990*

. . . .

Studies bear out that males as young as age thirteen think that if they are out on a date and spend a certain amount of money, they are entitled to certain things [such as sex].

—*Phyllis Pennese*

Don't ever make the mistake of trying to figure out what a man means when he says something. Parrots can string words together too.

—*Anonymous*

The best success rate in finagling a man into wearing a condom appears to be among those women who purchase their own—size extra large. Go ahead, let him think that smirk on your face is from ecstasy.

—*Dorian Yeager*

The great truth is that women
actually like men, and men can
never believe it.
—*Isabel Patterson, 1944*